Self Publishing College

- Notebook Size: 6*9 -

Self Publishing College
Tel: +886-2-2732-6526
Add: 6F.-6, No.63, Sec. 3, Heping E. Rd., Da'an Dist., Taipei City
106, Taiwan

www.ingramcontent.com/pod-product-compliance
Lightning Source LLC
Chambersburg PA
CBHW061501250726
48657CB00005B/1681